Deliverance for All Walks Of Life

Nancy Enyie

Deliverance for All Walks Of Life
Copyright © 2014 by Nancy Enyie

ISBN-13: 978-0692386194

Library of Congress Control Number: 2015904967

Scripture quotations taken from the Holy Bible, King James Version

Dedication

This book is dedicated to all different walks of life.

Table of Contents:

Table of Contents:

Table of Contents:

Table of Contents:

Yea, though I walk through the valley of the shadow of death, I will fear no evil: for thou art with me; thy rod and thy staff they comfort me.

Psalms 23:4

Lion's Den

Your enemy's appearance may look different, but the experience of either is deadly to the flesh. Remember when Daniel was thrown in the lion's den. God shut the lion's mouth, but when Daniel's enemies were thrown in, they became lunch. There is danger or protection according to what side you are on (God or the enemy).

1 Peter 5:8
 Be sober, be vigilant; because your adversary the devil, as a roaring lion, walketh about, seeking whom he may devour.

Believe

Never lose hope when it looks like it is hopeless. Believe that Jesus said unto them, I am the resurrection, and the life: he that believeth in me, though he were dead, yet shall he live: And whosoever liveth and believeth in me shall never die. Believest thou this? (John 11:25-26)

Who report will you believe? You will become the report that you are willing to believe (good or bad.)

John 11:25
Jesus said unto her, I am the resurrection, and the life: he that believeth in me, though he was dead, yet shall he live.

Deliverance Agreement

Praise the Lord!!! God said, "You are not forgotten, and your answer is now Praise the Lord." I would like to touch and decree to agree with you in the name of Jesus. There is nothing too hard for God. His ears are open to answer His children's prayers, and we thank you right now Jesus for your healing, your protection, your peace, your favor, and your guidance. We speak against anything that the enemy is coming against us with in Jesus' name, and we cancel any assignment that the devil has in store. We cancel them now in Jesus' name. May the blood of Jesus cover you and your family like never before, in Jesus' name. Amen.

Psalms 34:15
The eyes of the LORD are upon the righteous, and his ears are open unto their cry.

Love

True love determines how much you love others. Love thy neighbor as thyself. Who is my neighbor? Those that do His will. For some, it is easier to say I love you than it is to show love. Jesus said, "Watch what you do, and not what you say." Share love! Share Jesus!

Luke 6:32
For if ye love them which love you, what thank have ye? For sinners also love those that love them.

Seek God's Heart

When you are seeking God only for His hands, you will
continue to be disappointed. God said, "Those that come to
Him must believe that He is a rewarder to those when we
earnestly seek Him (relationship with Him) not His hand,
but His heart. Your mouth is what He sees, but your heart is
what He hears. God is King, but not Burger King; you can't
have it your way, but you can have everything that He
promises His way. (Hebrews 11:6) God rewards those who
earnestly seek Him. The Lord's good promises to Israel did
not fail; all of His promises were fulfilled (Joshua 21:45).

Hebrews 11:6
But without faith it is impossible to please him: for he that
cometh to God must believe that he is, and that he is a
rewarder of them that diligently seek him.

Don't Water Down Your Seeds

You reap what you sow; whatsoever you sow will grow.
You reap what you sow; just because it hasn't manifested at
this time does not mean it won't. Remember, a seed takes
time to grow. Be careful not to plant weeds (doubt),
because they will take over your seed (belief). Some seeds
have been planted for years by being watered with unbelief.
Bad morals will corrupt good seeds. In order for your seed
to grow, you have to go by what you say and not what you
see. What you don't see will grow when you believe.

Matthews 13:32
Which indeed is the least of all seeds: but when it is grown,
it is the greatest among herbs, and becometh a tree, so that
the birds of the air come and lodge in the branches thereof.

God Plans

The devil has employees, and they work overtime (for our souls); that's their only purpose, but we are God's employees. God gave us a plan for our lives. We are in charge of our destination. God gave us authority over our enemy in Jesus' name. Do not allow the enemy to steal what you are employed (stand) for.

Jeremiah 29:11
For I know the thoughts that I think toward you, saith the LORD, thoughts of peace, and not of evil, to give you an expected end.

Wait for the Harvest

When you are connected to change, there is no way your life will remain the same. A seed needs time to grow. A farmer can plow his field, fertilize it, but he still has to wait for the harvest. In the meantime, don't allow your weeds to take over your harvest before it's ready with unbelief and doubt. (Galatians 6:9)

Galatians 6:9
And let us not be weary in well doing: for in due season we shall reap if you faint not.

Hearing from God

Have you ever wondered, will God answer your prayers? It can be summed up into one question: Do you hear Him? Once you answer the question, you will have your answer. My sheep hear my voice, and I know them, and they follow Me. (John 10:27)

John 10:27
My sheep hear my voice, and I know them, and they follow me.

Our Daily Dose

This is our daily dose (The Bible). If you miss a dose, take it immediately. Our savior is our daily bread; without it we will starve ourselves to death. Let's eat more of it (His Word) so that we will stay full of it (His Spirit). In John 6:51, Jesus said, "I am the living bread that came down from heaven; if anyone eats of this bread, he will live forever."

John 6:51
I am the living bread which came down from heaven: if any man eat of this bread, he shall live forever: and the bread that I will give is my flesh, which I will give for the life of the world.

A Spiritual Trial

Whenever you are in a spiritual trial, don't give up and throw in the towel. You are on the battlefield, and you're covered up under His will. There is no way out of the fight; if you give up, you lose your rights. Fight the good fight of faith. Faith without work is dead; have faith and be spiritually lead.

James 2:14
What doth it profit, my brethren, through a man say he hath faith, and have not works? Can faith save him?

The Alarm

Sound the alarm, the word of God is at hand.
God watches over, and no one can take over Him (Jesus).
The devil couldn't kill Him.
The little king couldn't rule Him.
The people couldn't fool Him.
And Judas's kiss didn't surprise Him.
The grave couldn't hold Him.
Your chains have been broken by Him.
Pray for the ones that deny Him.

Answered Prayers

And it shall come to pass, that before they call, I will
answer; and while they are yet speaking, I will hear.
(Isaiah 65:24) So if you have not yet received an answer,
wait patiently for it. It will surely come to pass.

Philippians 4:19
But my God shall supply all your need according to his
riches in glory by Christ Jesus.

The Power Within

We have the power within. Don't worry about the chain someone is trying to hold you down with. We have that unshakeable, unstoppable faith, and favor. We've have the firepower of the Holy Spirit. The more they try to handcuff us, the more we break free. The more they pour water on us, the hotter we get. We're just like that burning bush; people look at us and wonder why we aren't burned up or out. They don't understand we've have a burning fire on the inside. We are burning, but not consumed.

Deuteronomy 4:24
For the LORD thy God is a consuming fire, even a jealous God.

Unbearable Pain

When your pain seems so unbearable, and it seems like
God doesn't care, and your situation turns out much
different than you planned, remember: God does care, and
your pain He does share. Your pain is part of your progress
to get you in God's plans and His success for your life.
Remember what JESUS went through; the pain and shame
it was for you. So, no matter what you are facing, you can
come through, because JESUS love for you has already
come through for you. Therefore, you will come through
also; you are not alone. Remember, JESUS after His pain:
He has risen, and you too will rise above your pain.

Isaiah 61:7
For your shame ye shall have double; and for confusion
they shall rejoice in their portion.

Your Certificate

Jesus called twelve disciples to teach them to be what He called for them to be. Jesus gave them their certificates before they even graduated. They couldn't earn the certificates by their works, but by The One that called them. The world certificates are useless, but when God certifies you, they are priceless. No one can disqualify what God qualifies.

Philippians 3:14
I press toward the mark for the prize of the high calling of God in Christ Jesus.

God's Timing

Sometimes God's plans don't work out as fast as we plan for them. We would like for our plans to work out in our timing. God's timing is not ours, and our timing is not God's timing. God knows our plans; He also knows our purpose and the time of our blessing. As we discover (the unknown to be known), we are to wait with patience as we discover our God, and His answers are all in His timing. Everything God promises and plans for our lives, even though it tarries, wait for it. It shall surely come to pass (Habakkuk 2:3).

Habakkuk 2:3
For the vision is yet for an appointed time, but at the end it shall speak, and not lie: though it tarry, wait for it; because it will surely come, it will not tarry.

Jesus our True Calling

Jesus is our true calling. He is our shield and butler. Jesus said, "All power has been given to Him. Without the Son is like being without the Father; you can't have one without the other." They are both one, and we are one in them. So, no matter how many gifts you are working with, there is no one greater. We are all one in Christ. There is no reason for anyone to boast or even be jealous, but be grateful.

Psalms 28:7
The LORD is my strength and my shield; my heart trusted in him, and I am helped: therefore my heart greatly rejoiceth; and with my song will I praise him.

Rise

Rise and shine for the glory of God has risen upon your situation. Rise above disappointment; God doesn't need your resume for a position. He qualifies you by your faith. He said, "According to your faith, let it be done unto you." (Matthew 9:29)

Matthew 9:29
According to your faith let it be done unto you.

Escape Plan

The devil always has a plot and a plan, but God always has an escape plan. God is faithful. There hath no temptation taken you but such as is common to man: but God is faithful, who will not suffer you to be tempted above that ye are able; but will with the temptation also make a way to escape, that ye may be able to bear it. (1Corinthians 10:13)

1 Corinthians 10:13
There hath no temptation taken you but such as is common to man: but God is faithful, who will not suffer you to be tempted above that ye are able; but will with the temptation also make a way to escape, that ye may be able to bear it.

A God Idea

Make sure your good idea is a God idea.
One day of pleasure without Jesus can cost you a lifetime
of pain. There is fun in pleasure, but the pay-back is pain. If
you don't die to yourself, whether it's good or bad, you will
become what you love. Just knowing Jesus is not good
enough, but accepting Him is.

No Respect of Person

Who is Jesus to you? You can never receive anything if you only see Jesus through what He is doing in other people's lives. God is no respect of persons. Start seeking him for yourself. Know that you are healed, wealthy, healthy, and an overcomer. Let Jesus be all that He is in you. As a man thinks, so is he. All you will ever need, you will find within you.

James 2:1
My brethren, have not the faith of our Lord Jesus Christ, the Lord of glory, with respect of persons.

Hungry or Thirsty

Does anyone feel a little hungry or thirsty? Jesus said, "I am the bread of life. The one who comes to me will never go hungry, and the one who believes in me will never be thirsty." (John 6:35)

Matthew 5:6
Blessed are they which do hunger and thirst after righteousness: for they shall be filled.

Imperfect

This is for someone who feels like everything you do, you just can't get it right. You say I was doing well, and I fell again. Be encouraged. We are imperfect people, in an imperfect world, with imperfect families, with imperfect relationships, and an imperfect situation. We have a perfect solution: Jesus. We can never be good enough, but in Jesus we are perfect. (Holy) (Matthew 5:48)

Matthews 5:48
Be ye therefore perfect, even as your Father which is in heaven is perfect.

God's Love

Romans 5:8

But God commendeth his love toward us, in that, while we
were yet sinners, Christ died for us. There is nothing we
can do to earn God's love; just accept it.

A smile is better than a frown.
To encourage is better than to discourage.
You are not a victim, but you are victorious.
You have not been put down, but planted.
You have not been left out, but picked out.

Good News

You may be hurt, disappointed, lonely, and feeling down right now, but there is good news (God). Your feeling is not your day; the way people treat you is not your day; but the joy of the Lord is. The reason people want to put you down is that they are too afraid to step where God is taking you. Therefore, they want to keep you from where they feel like they will never go (Higher).

Nehemiah 8:10
The Joy of the Lord is my strength.

The Power of Love

Love is more powerful than hate.
Faith is more powerful than fear.
Can is more powerful than can't.
Strong is more powerful than weak.
Light is more powerful than darkness
God is more powerful than Satan.
We are more powerful than what we will ever face.
We have all power within; it is called the Holy Ghost
Power. (Acts 1:8)

Facing Hard Times

When we are facing hard times, look at it as our learning time. You find out who are with you, who your friends are, and who your enemies are. We live, learn, and trust in Jesus through all our ups and downs in life.

Proverbs 18:24
A man that hath friends must shew himself friendly: and there is a friend that sticketh closer than a brother.

Your Struggle

In your struggle, that's where you will find out how strong you really are. What you have already gone through and survived, when you felt as though it was going to take you out, God gave you the strength and brought you through. So whatever struggles you are facing right now, you are stronger than your struggle with Jesus.

2 Corinthians 12:9
And he said unto me, My grace is sufficient for thee: for my strength is made perfect in weakness.

Dream Again

If your dream has died, let God's dream now live. Nothing around Him can stay dead. It's resurrection time in your life. Call those things in your life forth, even your loved ones (in Jesus' name come forth).

Luke 14:14
And thou shalt be blessed; for they cannot recompense thee: for thou shalt be recompensed at the resurrection of the just.

God's Promise

Whatever God promises us will come to pass. God didn't promise us our problem, but He did promise us a way to escape, perseverance, and endurance. Nevertheless, it seems like it's past time on our time, but with God, it is His promise and timing. God is not short concerning His promise, but we fall short waiting on it. Don't give up on the problem, but stay in the promise. Endure and it shall come to pass.

Hebrews 10:36
For ye have need of patience, that, after ye have done the will of God, ye might receive the promise.

Praise in Advance

Praise God in advance. It will help you overcome your circumstances. If you are feeling lonely and hurt right now, trust God. He will bring you out somehow. Don't worry if it has been long; keep praying and holding on. When you have been fighting for so long, keep Jesus you want to go wrong. If you feel like your strength is gone, and you are barely holding on, you will come through. God is not short of his promise; every word is true. Therefore, hold on to your hope, faith, vision, dream, and His strength when you feel as if you can't.

Luke 20:21
And they asked him, saying, Master, we know that thou sayest and teachest rightly, neither acceptest thou the person of any, but teachest the way of God truly:

Don't Waste Time on Your Enemy

Don't waste time on your enemy. People can't dictate your future when they are not the ones who gave it to you. They cannot change any plans they have not made. Therefore, stop worrying about your enemies; do not waste time on people who are not in your plans.

Jeremiah 29:11
For I know the thoughts that I think toward you, saith the LORD, thoughts of peace, and not of evil, to give you an expected end.

Your Chains are Broken

Jesus has set the captives free. Now the devil has to let you be. Your chains have been broken. No more will you be bound, Jesus has locked him down. Your way has been made; lift up your hands and give Him praise. You know the price He paid for three days, and there He lay, but on the third day, He was raised and our life He paid. Oh! What a celebration it will be when He comes back for all to see. Therefore, all the righteous will be glad, but for the enemies it will be sad.

John 8:36
If the Son therefore shall make you free, ye shall be free indeed.

Walk Right

There is something wrong when someone doesn't want to walk with what's right, but continues to walk anyway. You will know who will be with you and who's going to go. You are there, but you will be hurt when you find out who's not there with you. No matter how much, you have put your trust in them, only to find out how quickly it can be shattered, and your trust broken. Wounds do heal, and new friends He will reveal to those that do His will. True friends stand together, and nothing will cause them to stumble. (Romans 14:13) Do not cause another to stumble (John 15:14-15); Jesus called us friend.

Romans 14:13
Let us not therefore judge one another anymore: but judge this rather, that no man put a stumbling block or an occasion to fall in his brother's way.

No Excuse

I know we are under grace, but we are not under excuse. Be ye holy for I am holy. (1Peter 1:16; Leviticus 11:44) Only the righteous shall see God. (Matthew 5:8) Jesus is our example. (1 Corinthian 11:1)

No temptation has taken us that He has not made a way for us to escape. (1Corinthians-10:13)

God did not promise us that we wouldn't have trouble, but He did promise us that, through Jesus, we can overcome. (John 16:33)

John 16:33
These things I have spoken unto you, that in me ye might have peace. In the world ye shall have tribulation: but be of good cheer; I have overcome the world.

The Role

Don't just appear to be righteous. Life is not a rehearsal; you don't play the script (the word), you live it. Some people want to play the role besides being the role. Your friends, teachers, leaders, and church people can out shout the best of us, out dress the rest of us, preach longer than most of us. Playing a role is for peoples, but being the role is unto Christ. If you play, you pay not your way, but His. Even so, ye also outwardly appear righteous unto men, but within ye are full of hypocrisy and iniquity. (Matthew 23:28)

2 Corinthians 4:16
For which because we faint not; but though our outward man perish, yet the inward man is renewed day by day.

Faith

Believe that God is your rewarder. Faith is the evidence of things not seen but hoped for. If you have faith as a mustard seed, your faith can remove your mountain. Your faith is your proof of whose report you will believe. Your faith will pay off if you faint not. Fight the good fight of faith; whatever God promises you, He is able to fulfill. Be ye encouraged. Faith is not what you see, it is not what you have, but it is what you believe.

Hebrew 11:1
Now faith is the substance of things hoped for, the evidence of things not seen.

Your Valley

Thank God for your valley. If you had never experienced your valley, you would never appreciate your mountains.

Luke 17:6
And the Lord said, "If ye had faith as a grain of mustard seed, ye might say unto this sycamine tree, be thou plucked up by the root, and be thou planted in the sea; and it should obey you."

Keep Your Fire Burning

Keep our oil light (burning). We as Christians have to keep our fire burning. Just like wood or gas, sooner or later it will burn out if you don't keep adding to it, and that's the way we are. We have to keep our tank (ourselves) full of His word. If not we will soon burn out. No firepower, only smoke will soon vanish. The foolish ones said unto the wise, Give us of your oil; for our lamps are gone out. But the wise answered, saying not so; least there be not enough for us and you: but go ye rather to them that sell, and buy for yourselves (Matthew 25:8, 9).

Matthew 5:14
Ye are the light of the world. A city that is set on an hill cannot be hid.

God Cares

God is not out to blame you. God is not out to shame you. God is out to let you know how much He cares, loves, and died for us all. While we were yet sinners, His love for us has never changed; but when we get His love in us, His love will change us, to live right, be right, know right, and die according to our right, and live according to his word.

1 John 4:16
And we have known and believed the love that God hath to us. God is love; and he that dwelleth in love dwelleth in God and God in him.

Shout for Joy

But let all those who put their trust in Thee rejoice; let them ever shout for joy, because Thou defend them; let them also that love Thy name be joyful in Thee. For Thou, Lord, wilts bless the righteous; with favor, wilt thou encompass him as with a shield. (Psalms 5:11-12)

The Battle Belongs to God

What you are facing or going through, I know it is a real battle, and it is no surprise to God. He already said, "The battle belongs to Him." The battle belongs to Him; we have to speak as if God was fighting the battle himself. If you talk defeat, you will be defeated. You have what you say, but if you want to see your enemy defeated, it will never happen in your own words, only His word (God). No matter how big your problem or your mountain might be, speak, say, and talk to God words on any situation, circumstance, or problem. You will have a turn-around on your behalf. You will overcome and recover all.

1 Samuel 17:47
And all this assembly shall know that the LORD saveth not with sword and spear; for the battle is the LORD'S, and He will give you into our hands."

Choose This Day

There is more to it than just reading our bible; you have to receive, believe, and obey. This is our everyday life. It will tell you where you stand now in your faith. It also tells us we have a choice every day. Choose this day whom you will serve. Through trial and pain, whose report are you going to believe: faithful as promised or little faith and forsaken?

Joshua 24:15
And if it seem evil unto you to serve the LORD, choose you this day whom ye will serve; whether the gods which your fathers served that were on the other side of the flood, or the gods of the Amorites, in whose land ye dwell: but as for me and my house, we will serve the LORD.

Moving out of God's Way

To see the miraculous move of God, we have to move (ourselves) out so God can move in. We have to step out so that God can order our steps. We have to walk so God can lead. We have to ask before God can answer. We have to speak His language so He will hear us.

Psalm 119:133
Order my steps in thy word: and let not any iniquity have dominion over me.

Trust in the Promise

When others don't approve of God's plans for your life, remember they didn't call you. Man goes by what he sees, and God goes by the unseen so that it can be seen. Trust in God, and you will see everything God promised will come to be presented.

Romans 4:17
(As it is written, I have made thee a father of many nations,) before him whom he believed, even God, who quickeneth the dead, and calleth those things which be not as though they were.

The Race

Keep the faith to run this race. You will get tired; just rest and pray for a while. God will give you the strength when you feel like you can't go any further. You will soon find out you are not alone. You have an encourager saying, "Stay strong." You can make it through. Don't quit no matter what you do. God will see you through.
Continue to run the race, because your victory day is coming.

Ecclesiastes 9:11
I returned, and saw under the sun, that the race is not to the swift, nor the battle to the strong, neither yet bread to the wise, nor yet riches to men of understanding, nor yet favour to men of skill; but time and chance

You Are

When you have been put down, let down, and looked down upon don't stay down. You are more than a conqueror; you are strong, you are valuable, you are special, you are cherished, you are treasured, you are chosen, you are loved beyond measure, and you are God's beloved. If you work well with what you have, God will no wise cast you out and (John 6:37), He will bring you out. (Remember the Parable of the ones that received talents.) Do well with what gifts you have.

Romans 8:37
Nay, in all these things we are more than conquerors through him that loved us.

When God Calls You

When God has called you, don't be amazed or find it strange. When you feel like no one understands you, and your friends are now few and family too. People are turning their backs on you, especially the ones you thought would be proud of you. The word said, how can two walk together unless they agree? For there is nothing covered, that shall not be revealed; neither hid, that shall not be known (Luke12:2).

Luke 12:2
For there is nothing covered, that shall not be revealed; neither hid, that shall not be

Unstoppable

We have unstoppable, unshakeable, unmovable, and unbelievable faith. The harder it gets the more we have to press. The more things shake us the more we have to shake it off because nothing can stay connected against us; no chains, no weapons, no words, no plots, no sicknesses, no storms, no disappointments, and no lies. Our enemies need to realize, we are anointed! Nevertheless, through our Messiah and His anointing will destroy every yoke. We are empowered within by our Savior. We are equipped (His armor) more than conquers (we are over comers) with His word, His power. We are His chosen.

Matthew 11:30
For my yoke is easy and my burden is light.

The Vision

Without a vision, my people perish not because they don't have a vision, but because they refuse to see. Have perseverance and never lose hope when everything is falling apart around you. When there is more pain than peace, remember God's word will never fail, and neither will His promise. In your pain, strength in Him you can gain. His promise is more than the pain you feel. Trust in Him and, you will see a change.

Proverbs 29:18
Where there is no vision, the people perish: but he that keepeth the law, happy is he.

Sinners

Jesus sat with sinners not to become one, but to let them know they didn't have to stay one. People need to see through the eyes of Jesus; then they will see love. Love thy neighbor as thyself. Who is my neighbor? Those that do His will.

Psalms 31:23
O love the LORD, all ye his saints: for the LORD preserveth the faithful, and plentifully rewardeth the proud doer.

Your Decision

Where you are now is not as important as where God is taking you. The decisions you make now in a temporary situation will determine the outcome of His promise. Whatever God promised you shall come to pass, and whatever storm you are facing, it will pass. Don't make a permanent decision on your own. Saul's kingdom was ripped from him. Do not let yours be ripped from you. Your dream, God promised. (1 Samuel 15:23, 27 -28)

Mark 4:39
And he arose, and rebuked the wind, and said unto the sea, Peace, be still. And the wind ceased, and there was a great calm.

Refreshed in the Spirit

Let the anointing fall upon you like the morning dew. Let it soak into your spirit. Fill yourself up to overflow with His Holy Spirit, and let the anointing destroy every yoke of bondage that would try so easily to entangle you, misguide you, and mislead you. Remember, we are not exempt from the enemy's wicked devices. We overcome them by the blood of the lamb and the word of our testimony.

Revelation 12:11
And they overcame him by the blood of the Lamb, and by the word of their testimony;

Don't Try to Fight the Battle

Don't try to fight a battle with your own strength. You will soon find out that you can't. The battle is not giving to the swift and strong or to those that try to fight alone. It was not meant for you to win; that is why Jesus paid for our sins, and without Him, you cannot win.

Ecclesiastic 9:11
I returned, and saw under the sun, that the race is not to the swift, nor the battle to the strong, neither yet bread to the wise, nor yet riches to men of understanding, nor yet favor to men of skill; but time and chance happened to them all.

Dream Again/Hope Again

If you feel like your dream has died. It's not too late dream again. If you have hope there is still time. When you have a desire, there is always a way. If your ways have failed you, and if people or a person has failed you, Jesus way will never fail or forsake you. JESUS is the truth and our way. God knows the plans He has for you, and if you put your trust in Him, He will see you through. His plans will never fail you.

John 14:16
Jesus saith unto him, I am the way, the truth, and the life: no man cometh unto the Father, but by me.

Made Up Mind

With perseverance, you can work your way through difficulties. Many are the afflictions of the righteous: but the LORD delivereth him out of them all. (Psalm 34:19)

Be encouraged; you can do it. I (you) can do all things through Christ which strengtheneth me. (Philippians 4:13)

Have a made up mind when you want to quit. Let this mind be in you, which was also in Christ Jesus: (Philippians 2:5)

Your enemy will help you get to your destination. After you see the tragedy of their life, you will want to change your life.

Power in the Word

There is power in the word of JESUS. Jesus did everything that you heard. He opened the eyes of the blind and they started seeing just fine. Jesus set the possessed free and the demons had to let him be. He even raised the dead all this by being spirit lead. There is power in His word and we can do all things that we heard, through His word!!

Roman 8:14
For as many as are led by the Spirit of God, they are the sons of God.

Spiritual Trial

Whenever you are in a spiritual trial, don't give up and throw in the towel. You are on the battle-field and you are covered by His will. There is no way out of the fight. If you give up, you lose your rights. Fight the good fight of faith. Faith without work is dead. Have faith and be spiritually lead.

1 Timothy 6:12
Fight the good fight of faith, lay hold on eternal life, whereunto thou art also called, and hast professed a good profession before many witnesses.

Extra Cleaning

Does anyone need some extra cleaning? Okay! Let us shower in His anointing, bathe in His spirit, and soak in His word. Now enjoy the sweet aroma of God's fragrance. There is nothing that can be compared to it.

Psalms 51:7
Purge me with hyssop, and I shall be clean: wash me and I shall be whiter than snow.

Die to Ourselves

We have to give up everything that we are in order to become everything that He is (Jesus). We have to die daily to ourselves, take up His cross, and follow Him. We can die to ourselves and live for Jesus or die for ourselves and die without Him.

Luke 9:23
And he said to them all, if any man will come after me, let him deny himself, and take up his cross daily, and follow me.

Hiding Place

The Lord is our hiding place. When we run to Him, we are safe no matter what is going on around us. He knows and sees everything people do. Don't let trouble keep you afraid. Just lift your hands and give Him some praise. He is a lifter of your head and He won't let you be misled.

Psalms 32:7
Thou art my hiding place; thou shalt preserve me from trouble; thou shalt compass me about with songs of deliverance. Selah.

Right Decision

Make a right decision no matter how wrong you are being treated. Don't become what they are. My God, your God, and our God will render to every man according to the works of His hands. It is God's way, not ours. We need to stay out of His way, and He will work it out.

Roman 2:6
Who will render to every man according to his deeds:

Devil Selling, Don't Buy In

The devil is always selling something; do not buy in no matter what you do. He doesn't look anything like his name sounds, because he comes in many smiles and frowns. It doesn't matter if you are a women, man, or child; if you let him, he will stay for a while (in your life). He doesn't care. Satan will destroy your child; all it takes for him is just a little while. He'll dress it up and make it look good to you. Otherwise, he knows he couldn't get through. Don't buy in or try in, but believe in (our Savior) and you won't get taken in

John 10:10
The thief cometh not, but for to steal, and to kill, and to destroy: I am come that they might have life, and that they might have it more abundantly.

Life Assurance

Do you have your fire assurance? People have car insurance, house insurance, but do you have life assurance? This is not something you can buy or try; get your fire protection plan today. "JESUS" has all the coverage's you need. To see your assurance and protection plans, open your contract, it's all written down. "Your Bible is your Life Assurance."

1 John 5:7
For there are three that bear record in heaven, the Father, the Word, and the Holy Ghost: and these three are one.

In Your Comfort Zone

When Jesus is in the boat with you, you are safe and protected. When you are in the boat and you are in your comfort zone and looking at the water saying, "I don't know if I can do this," you have to remember the one who was with you in the boat will be the same one with you out of the boat. You are never alone; you are walking by faith. Sometimes you have to let your faith take you, where your fear wants to keep you from. So when Jesus calls, step out of your comfort zone (the boat), and if you fall, Jesus will catch you and pull you up again.

2 Corinthians 5:7
For we walk by faith, not by sight.

Ezekiel 36:31- 32

Then shall ye remember your own evil ways, and your
doings that were not good, and shall lothe yourselves in
your own sight for your iniquities and for your
abominations. Not for your sakes do I this, saith the Lord
God, be it known unto you: be ashamed and confounded
for your own ways, O house of Israel.

Endure Perseverance

Endure perseverance. Things do happen in life that we cannot control, but God will give you strength to endure; however, you have to do it in His will. You have to do it in His strength, because the situation will be too much for you to carry. The weight of life will wear you out and down. That's why He said, "My yoke is easy and my burden is light." Ride on eagle wings when you are going through a storm hold on to perseverance. Stay steadfast and have unmovable faith, and you will overcome. This too shall pass. Praise God in advance. He will change your circumstance.

Matthew 11:30
For my yoke is easy, and my burden is light.

When you are Chosen

You are chosen, called, and anointed by God. When God
has given you a vision and a dream, He will bring it to pass.
God has given you His promised word; your promise is
going to look like everything except a promise. Your
promotion will eventually lead you to His promise,
therefore, whatever problem you will face, God has already
given you the solution.

Matthews 25:13
Watch therefore, for ye know neither the day nor the hour
wherein the Son of man cometh.

Your Story

The reason why you praise Him like you do, in spite of
how people look at you or what they think of you, is
because they don't understand your story and the pain He
has brought you through. Some people don't understand
His glory, so they will never understand your story. A
person is the reason you have a story and the enemy is the
reason for your pain. But God!

No Matter What

No matter what you are going through, and no matter what you are facing, keep your focus on Jesus and you can win this race, no matter what. There's power in His word. Work with what you've got; be faithful no matter what little you have. Little is better than none. Have faith in God. You can prosper in what you do. Believe in Jesus, everything He says is true. If you hold on to His word, He will bless you like no one has ever heard.

Luke16:10
He that is faithful in that which is least is faithful also in much: and he that is unjust in the least is unjust also in much.

Sit with Jesus

Jesus is our living Savior. Call on Him day or night, He's able. He is able to lift you up and bring you out with dancing, shouting, and running. Sit with Jesus and hear Him out. You will be amazed with what you will find out. He is able to bring everything He promised.

Ezekiel 20:34
And I will bring you out from the people, and will gather you out of the countries wherein ye are scattered, with a mighty hand, and with a stretched out arm, and with fury poured out.

If God Said It, It Is So

If God says so, it is so. You can't add to it or take away from it. If God says so, it is so; healing, peace, love, protection, purpose, and prosperity. You are the head and not the tail, to be above only and not beneath. Call those things that be not, as though they were. God has given you power to get wealth. He has His plans for us, in spite of what you are going through or facing. If God says so, it will be so. First (Believe), second (Receive), and third (Expect).

Matthew 5:37
But let your communication be, yea, yea; nay, nay:

Your Past

Everyone has a past, but you don't have to keep living it. Jeremiah 29:13 said, "And ye shall seek me, and find me, when ye shall search for me with all your heart."

Isaiah 43:18
Remember ye not the former things, neither consider the things of old.

Sick and Tired: (pick yourself up)

When you are sick and tired of yourself, maybe soon you will realize you've been the problem all along. Sometimes we are our worst critics. We don't need any help from other people. We do well all by ourselves, putting ourselves down. God didn't call you to put yourself down, but to lay your flesh down. So stop helping the enemy out; instead, start speaking: I am not weak, but strong. I am special, I am loved, and I am God's beloved. What a beautiful person I am. I am the apple of God's eye. I am fearfully and wonderfully made.
Let today be a start of a new beginning. Start decreeing and declaring God's Word over your life.

Job 22:28
Thou shalt also decree a thing, and it shall be established unto thee: and the light shall shine upon thy ways.

2 Peter 1:5-8

"And beside this, giving all diligence, add to your faith virtue; and to virtue knowledge; And to knowledge temperance; and to temperance patience; and to patience godliness; And to godliness brotherly kindness; and to brotherly kindness charity. For if these things be in you, and abound, they make you that ye shall neither be barren nor unfruitful in the knowledge of our Lord Jesus Christ."

One Accord

The bible is like a courtroom, there is only one judge, and we are like the jury: we must be on one accord.

Acts 1:14
These all continued with one accord in prayer and supplication, with the women, and Mary the mother of Jesus, and with his brethren.

Challenges in Life

Jesus is the reason for every season. This is your season now; don't face your challenges as being hard with Jesus, but as if you have already conquered them. There is no way you can live life without facing some difficulties, and there is no way you can overcome them without Jesus.

Deuteronomy 11:14
That I will give *you* the rain of your land in his due season, the first rain and the latter rain, that thou mayest gather in thy corn, and thy wine, and thine oil.

Finished Product

Just like making a cake, the ingredients never look like what it will turn out to be: the finished product. God is well able to finish what He has begun in you: good works. Just because your problem does not look like your promise, it is because all the ingredients have to be put together for your good. Now you know how valuable your promise is. You will know all the ingredients you went through to get it.

Philippians 1:6
Being confident of this very thing, that he which hath begun a good work in you will perform it until the day of Jesus Christ:

Never Alone

Life sometimes makes you feel like you are the only one climbing the mountain, until you look back and see that others are also heading where you are going. You are never alone; it is a feeling, not a fact.

Deuteronomy 31:6
Be strong and of a good courage, fear not, nor be afraid of them: for the LORD thy God, he it is that doth go with thee; he will not fail thee, nor forsake thee.

Build Yourself Up

Jesus is our living word. We have life in Him. Words are very powerful; use your words wisely. You can build yourself up, or you can tear yourself down. Do not let anyone build you up. Believe in yourself first. Sometimes the one who builds you up can be the one who will tear you down. Build yourself upon the Rock (God's Word). When a man motivates you, he will bring it up, but when God motivates, He elevates and brings you up.
Let God motivate you and not man.

Hebrews 4:12
For the word of God is quick, and powerful, and sharper than any two-edged sword, piercing even to the dividing asunder of soul and spirit, and of the joints and marrow, and is a discerner of the thoughts and intents of the heart.

Having Faith

One thing about faith is, you can stand with a person in faith. You cannot believe for them, but with them. The word said, "According to your faith, be it unto you." (Matthew 9:29) Tragedy sometimes will have you weak and wounded, but God can work with your faith if you ask, "Lord help thou mine unbelief." (Mark 9:24) God cannot help you with anything you are not willing to confess.

Matthew 9:29
"According to your faith, be it unto you."

Not Forgotten

Praise the Lord. God said, "You are not forgotten, and your answer is now, Praise the Lord." I just wanted to touch and decree to agree in the name of Jesus. There is nothing too hard for God. His ears are open to answer His children's prayers, and we thank you right now, Jesus, for your healing, protection, peace, favor, and guidance. In Jesus' name, we bind all the attacks that the enemy has planned, and we cancel any assignment the devil has in store. Thank you, God, for the blood of Jesus covering you, your family, my family, and me, like never before. In Jesus' name, Amen.

Job 22:28
Thou shalt also decree a thing, and it shall be established unto thee: and the light shall shine upon thy ways.

His Glory

If people do not know your pain, people can never understand your praise, your story, or His glory. Let's stick to the basics: The Bible. The only reason Jesus came is so that we can live. It is time for ministries to stop coming for just the gathering, but for Jesus. Church is not for entertainment, but for eternal life.

John 3:16
For God so loved the world, that he gave his only begotten Son, that whosoever believeth in him should not perish, but have everlasting life.

Don't Just Advertise

Don't just snack on the word, but eat the entire meal. A snack will help you get by, but a full meal will help you overcome. Snacks are just appetizers, but the full meal shows the evidence. Remember the fig tree: it advertised but had no fruit.

Mark 11:14
And Jesus answered and said unto it, No man eat fruit of thee thereafter forever. And his disciples heard it.

Ephesians 5:17, 27

Wherefore be ye not unwise, but understanding what the will of the Lord is. That he might present it to himself a glorious church, not having spot, or wrinkle, or any such thing; but that it should be holy and without blemish.

Your Struggle

In your struggle, that is where you will find out how strong you really are. What you have been through, you survived. When the struggle felt as if it was going to take you out, God gave you strength and brought you through. Jesus is still your strength; when you feel that you do not have the answer He will show you how. Whatever struggle you are facing right now, remember that you are stronger than your struggle with Jesus.

Deuteronomy 31:6
Be strong and of a good courage, fear not, nor be afraid of them: for the LORD thy God, he it is that doth go with thee; he will not fail thee, nor forsake thee.

Family Starts Acting Strange

When your family starts acting strange, then you notice a sudden change. When your in-laws start behaving like out-laws, I know it will be hard to cope, but with God there is still hope.

Romans 12:12
Rejoicing in hope; patient in tribulation; continuing instant in prayer;

Faith is stronger

Faith is stronger than fear.

Encourage is stronger than discourage.

Strength is stronger than weakness.

Love is more powerful than hate.

Jesus' word is more.

We have to speak what we want, and not let our ears hear and listen to what others are saying.

A Move Sometimes Isn't Easy

Sometimes making a Godly move is not always easy but necessary. God always knows best; that is why when we cannot, through Him we can. We are made stronger in our weakness. We can do all things with His strength. Make the move; you are stronger than what you are feeling. Lock your faith (strength) in, and kick your feeling (doubt) out.

2 Corinthians 12:19
Again, think ye that we excuse ourselves unto you? We speak before God in Christ: but we do all things, dearly beloved, for your edifying.

Phenomenal

There is a phenomenal move of God upon His people: we are royalty, we are children of the most high King, and we are valuable. Thank God for blessing us beyond our expectations. Stand strong and stay firm on His word. We are a royalty.

Without God

When you think you've got it going on, without God in it, you will go wrong. You yourself can't hear the Spirit saying go right. Right is what you should hear, but with the flesh it is not clear. When God is in control of your life, He saves you from others fleshly advice, when you let him lead. Don't worry about who believes in you, because what they don't know about you God will show. Even though it doesn't seem like things are moving along, you hold onto faith and stay strong. If you don't know it, you might blow it. When you start trying to make it happen you will not like the result.

Luke 1:37
For with God nothing shall be impossible.

Faith Fight

You are in a faith fight, and it is already fixed so that you will win. It may look like the enemy is winning. Know the fight was planned in advance. The coach and the referee, they are part of the plan. The referee is letting you know you can get up with every move the enemy hits you with. The coach is telling you that, you are more than a conqueror, you can do it. The fight was planned in advance you just had to step into the ring to make the fight complete. You fight with your heart not with your hands.

1 Timothy 1:12
And I thank Christ Jesus our Lord, who hath enabled me, for that he counted me faithful, putting me into the ministry;

Doing It God's Way

The do's and the don'ts will get you something you don't want in life. If you do it God's way, you will get God's results for your life, but if you do it your way, you will get your results. See, it is not what you buy, but it is the result of paying for doing the do's and don'ts your way (destruction, destroyed, your destitution).
The do is doing things God's way.
The do not is doing things your way.

Delivery from a Broken Mind Set

Sometimes when a person is broke, they don't always need money, but deliverance out of their broken mind-set and their broken thinking. As a man thinks, so is he. In the book of Acts, there was a beggar; he was asking for something he wanted. God gave him something he needed: deliverance. (Acts 3:5-6)

The lame man looked at them eagerly, expecting some money. Then Peter said, "Silver and gold have I none; but such as I have give I unto thee: In the name of Jesus Christ of Nazareth rise up and walk." (Acts 3:5)

Thank God for a new mind set. Roman 12:2

Continue to Speak His Word

A person have the wrong job if they do not follow the Father's instructions when teaching His word. It is not always going to be about what we want to hear, but it is what we need to know.

You are God's beloved and His word is planted in you, so continue to speak the word and grow.

Zechariah 2:8
For thus saith the LORD of hosts; After the glory hath he sent me unto the nations which spoiled you: for he that toucheth you toucheth the apple of his eye.

Complete Change

If you want to see a complete change in your life, give your life fully to Jesus. You will be so full in Him, there will not be enough room for anything else.

Ephesians 2:20
And are built upon the foundation of the apostles and prophets, Jesus Christ himself being the chief cornerstone;

Church is Not a Secret Place

The church is not a hiding place, but a healing place. The church is not a secret service. Once you get out of the building, tell others to build them up so that they may be added to the church not the building, but Christ.

And they, continuing daily with one accord in the temple, and breaking bread from house to house, did eat their meat with gladness and singleness of heart. (Acts 2:46)

Then saith He unto His disciples, "The harvest truly is plenteous, but the labourers are few." (Matthew 9:37)

Can You Bear This Cup?

Jesus asked, "Are you able to drink from this cup?" A person will say yes, but they want to put their own stuff in it. Jesus didn't say add to it but to bear through it. Jesus will help you to bear his cup, but not one will choose. (Matthew 20:22)

But Jesus answered and said, "Ye know not what ye ask. Are ye able to drink of the cup that I shall drink of, and to be baptized with the baptism that I am baptized with?" They say unto Him, "We are able." (Matthew 20:22)

Blow Ye This Trumpet

Blow ye the trumpet in Zion, and sound an alarm in my holy mountain: let all the inhabitants of the land tremble, for the day of the Lord cometh, for it is nigh at hand. (Joel 2:1)

But of that day and that hour knoweth no man, no, not the angels which are in heaven, neither the Son, but the Father. (Mark 13:32)

Benchwarmer

You know, we have more benchwarmers than feet steppers. More people are sitting down than being disciples. God called us not to be served, but to serve as He washed the disciples' feet. We are supposed to do likewise; to wash them, not to look down on them.

Luke 14:23
And the lord said unto the servant, Go out into the highways and hedges, and compel *them* to come in, that my house may be filled.

Believe that God is Your Rewarder

Faith is the evidence of things not seen, but yet hoped for; if you have faith the size of a mustard seed, your faith can remove your mountain.
Your faith is your proof of whose report you will believe.
Your faith will pay off. If you faint not, fight the good fight of faith. Whatever God promised you, He is able to fulfill.
Be ye encouraged: faith is not what you see.
Faith is not what you have.
Faith is what you believe.

An Open Book Test

The bible is the only test that no one will have an excuse not to pass; it's an open book test, and it will let you know when you mess up. All you have to do is correct and repent. It is the only open book test that will always give you the answers. Failure is not an option, but a choice.

Don't fail the life and death test. Failure is not an option but a choice. It is an open book test. You can do it, just obey (the bible).

All scripture is given by inspiration of God and is profitable for doctrine, for reproof, for correction, for instruction in righteousness. 2 Timothy 3:16

Age is an Option

Age is just an option; don't ever let it define your ability of what you can or can't do. If you are saying it's past your time, your dream, your vision, your health, in Jesus' name I am saying it's time for it to come to pass in Jesus' name.

Ecclesiastes 5:7
For in the multitude of dreams and many words there are also divers vanities: but fear thou God.

Your Elevation

Praise God, my brothers and sisters. Your eviction is your elevation to go to your next level higher in God. He is going to get glory out of this; what looks like your disaster is your deliverance. What looks like your problem will turn out to be God's promise. As of now, don't worry, take God at His word. Praise God, my sisters and brothers, praise Him. Praise Him, and rest in His peace, my sisters and brothers. All things are going to work out for your good.

Romans 8:28
And we know that all things work together for good to them that love God, to them who are the called according to *his* purpose.

But God

If people do not understand your story, they will never understand your praise. You might be this person: a person who praises, a person who shouts, a worshipper, or a joyful person. Some people will look at you strangely because they never understand your praise, but let it be unto God.

Rightfully Yours

Do not just settle for getting by; instead, take over what is rightfully yours (peace, joy, happiness, marriage, or health). With Jesus, you do not have to settle with just getting by, but taking over what God has promised you. You are over your enemy.

Today, claim back what is rightfully yours.

Proverbs 29:2
When the righteous are in authority, the people rejoice: but when the wicked beareth rule, the people mourn.

Get Over

Get over and not be taken over. You have to walk in it: Authority! You have to believe in your dream, your blessing, and always stand on God's word. If you want to love right, live right, and be right, let go of the old you and become the new you in Jesus.

Matthew 8:9
For I am a man under authority having soldiers under me; and I say to this man, Go, and he goeth; and to another, Come, and he cometh; and to my servant, Do this, and he doeth it.

Decisions

Good habits create good decisions, and bad habits create bad results. If you do it long enough, you will become what you do; good or bad, your life depends on it. You choose!

Joshua 24:14
Now therefore fear the LORD, and serve him in sincerity and in truth: and put away the gods which your fathers served on the other side of the flood, and in Egypt; and serve ye the LORD.

Love

To give love you need to have love. You cannot give
something that you do not have. You can have love if you
receive it, and you will know that you have it. If you can
believe in it, you can have it (love), you can receive it, and
you can know it if you believe in Love.

1 John 4:8
He that loveth not knoweth not God; for God is love.

Your Yes

You know when you see a post that reads, "Say Yes if you love Jesus." The answer is shown in your "Yes." How you love one another will determine how much you love Jesus. This question was asked to Peter three times: "Do you love me?"

1 John 4:7
Beloved, let us love one another: for love is of God; and every one that loveth is born of God, and knoweth God

Sacrifice

When Abraham's sacrifice was supplied, he took his son out of obedience, but he didn't know how God was going to do it (the sacrifice). Moses also trusted God in spite of not knowing God's plan. God said, "It's time for my people to come out of poverty and get into prosperity."

Genesis 22:8
And Abraham said, My son, God will provide himself a lamb for a burnt offering: so they went both of them together.

Accept it Now

If you cannot accept prosperity and your mansion here, you will be very disappointed when you get to heaven, but if you do not believe earthly things, how can you believe heavenly things. (John 3:12)

John 14:2
In my Father's house are many mansions: if it were not so, I would have told you. I go to prepare a place for you.

Willing Heart

I cannot talk you into your blessing; if I do, that means that someone else can come along and talk you out of your blessing, especially, if you do not have faith. God said, "If you have a willing heart you shall eat the good of the land."

Roman 11:20
Well; because of unbelief they were broken off, and thou standest by faith. Be not highminded, but fear:

Correction

Some people are settling for second best and some even
less. They don't need condemning, but correction. For
whom the Lord loveth he chasteneth, and scourgeth every
son who he receiveth. Hebrew 12:6/Acts 17:11

(Matthew 7:3-5)

If they don't take heed to correction, then God will
condemn them. Judge not and you won't be judge.
And why beholdest thou the mote that is in thy brother's
eye, but considerest not the beam that is in thine own eye?

Or how wilt thou say to thy brother, Let me pull out the
mote out of thine eye; and, behold, a beam is in thine own
eye?

Thou hypocrite, first cast out the beam out of thine own
eye; and then shalt thou see clearly to cast out the mote out
of thy brother's eye.

Everything around a change will change. Urge your brother
and sister.

Just Believe

The old saying is, "Jesus didn't have a mansion down here." This was because He was going back to His mansion. Did He not say, "I became poor so that through me you may become rich," and that's in everything including your faith? If you can't see prosperity, you can't ever have it. Jesus said, "The poor you will have with you always." They are too poor to believe that all things are possible.

Mark 14:7
For ye have the poor with you always, and whatsoever ye will ye may do them good: but me ye have not always.

Understanding

You cannot get anything or receive anything that you do not understand. Jesus said, "Have I not been so long and you yet without understanding." Some people looked at Jesus as if they did not understand, so He had to bag up what He brought up. (Matthew 15:16)

Right Move

There are many followers of God, but they may not be making the right move of God. They are moving in the right direction, but making some wrong decisions.

Psalms 37:5.
Commit thy way unto the LORD; trust also in him; and he shall bring *it* to pass.

Your Enemies

One thing about your enemies: they can never stop from reaching your destination, but they will slow you down if you take notice of them.

Philippians 3:14
I press toward the mark for the prize of the high calling of God in Christ Jesus.

Roaring Lion

Your enemies are just like a roaring lion, but do not let that intimidate you because when they open their mouths, it is just for them to yawn. (Remember Daniel 16:16-24)
Open your mouth and speak God's word to your situation!

Do not agree with your enemy.

Pleasure

There is fun in pleasure, but the payback is pain.

God is calling prayer warriors; He does not need prayer worriers. Pray and believe in His word; do not pray and still not believe.

Matthew 6:25
Therefore I say unto you, take no thought for your life, what ye shall eat, or what ye shall drink; nor yet for your body, what ye shall put on. Is not the life more than meat, and the body than raiment?

Don't Waste Time

Why waste time on your adversaries (your player haters), when they are not part of your plan. They are positioned or placed there to see how much place you will give them.

John 10:10
The thief cometh not, but for to steal, and to kill, and to destroy: I am come that they might have life, and that they might have it more abundantly.

It's a Fixed Fight

It may look like the enemy is winning; know the fight was planned in advance. You just had to step into the fight to make the fight complete. You are in a faith fight, and it is already fixed for you to win.

Know that you are a winner in Jesus' name.

Romans 8:37
Nay, in all these things we are more than conquerors through him that loved us.

Going Through

What looks like your tragedy is your triumph. What looks like trash to you could be your treasure to God. What looks like the ending to you is your beginning to God. What looks like a mess to you will turn out to be your message. After what you went through, you do not look like the evidence of your mess. When it looks like it's all over, remember Mordecai (Ester's uncle). God is just flipping the strip on the enemy. What the Devil meant for evil, God will turn it around for your good.

Don't Worry in Your Struggle

Don't worry about your life struggles, or if a change doesn't come soon. You will be elevated if you will trust God in your situation with praise and a shout. You have to do something different than what you feel, which is called Faith. You are not alone; remember the Hebrew Boys: what looked like a disaster was their deliverance. Your eviction is your elevation, God's ways are not our ways. What looks to us like an ending with Him is a beginning. Remember: the Red Sea didn't open up before they got there, but it wasn't time for the departure to take place until they stretched their faith forth.

No more worrying, but believing.

Stone Throwers

Don't worry about your stone throwers. Jesus paid for every stone your haters can ever throw at you. None of their words, plots, or weapons shall prosper.

If anyone dares to challenge you, it will not be my doing! Whoever tries to challenge you will be defeated. Behold, they shall surely gather together, but not by me: whosoever shall gather together against thee shall fall for thy sake. No weapon that is formed against thee shall prosper; and every tongue that shall rise against thee in judgment thou shalt condemn. This is the heritage of the servants of the LORD, and their righteousness is of me, saith the LORD (Isaiah 54:15, 17).

Psalms 35:1
Plead my cause, O LORD, with them that strive with me: fight against them that fight against me.

Be Anointed

To be anointed by God is not only to be picked, but also to be empowered by Him. The task or position to which He has called you.

Love Covers

Love covers a multitude of sin. Not for you to cover or keep, but to forsake.

Notes:

Notes:

Notes:

Notes:

www.ingramcontent.com/pod-product-compliance
Lightning Source LLC
LaVergne TN
LVHW051643080426
835511LV00016B/2457